High Wire

High Wire

Poems by

Stephen Anderson

Cover design by Shay Culligan
Cover image by Vashti Anderson
Author photo by Shlomo Godder

ISBN: 978-1-63980-057-5

Kelsay Books
502 South 1040 East, A-119
American Fork, Utah 84003
Kelsaybooks.com

Acknowledgments

Southwest Review: "Copper Dream"

Verse-Virtual: "Fisherman X"

Twist In Time: "Sojourn in Panama"

In The Garden Of Angels And Demons: "Song of Graffiti," "On the Road to Mayo," "In Style," "Things Said"

The Dream Angel Plays The Cello: "The Call," "The Bearable Light of Invisibility," "Quest," "On Stargazing," "Ascent," "At Dusk," "The Wait"

Your Daily Poem: "Thessaloniki's All in a Row," "The Ancient Art of War in the Garden"

The Silent Tango of Dreams: "On a Hot Afternoon in Jerusalem," "The Privileged Secrets of the Arch," "On the Glade Near Strawberry Fields,"

Navigating in the Sun: "Reverie," "Muted"

Verse Wisconsin: "Reminiscence on a Sunday Afternoon"

Poetica Review: "The Swerve"

Life and Legends: "Empty House," "Shifting Gears"

Lothlorien Poetry Journal: "the forge," "Time is a curious messenger," "Day Token," "burnt roses,"

Blue Heron Review: "Threads of a Dream"

Contents

Not everything that is faced can be changed, but nothing can be changed until it is faced.

—James Baldwin

Empty House

The other night
I dreamt I visited Isla Negra
but Neruda was not there. Only
formations of strange seabirds
skittered the sky above, rocks
whispered secret things of protest,
& the sea waves
spoke in tongues that burned clear
through my heart there outside the poet's
maritime palace ransacked by Pinochet's
marionettes ages ago in search of truths
they could never understand. I dreamt
that the tree I sat under dropped leaves
with poems written in blood-red ink. I
caressed the lush earth there, & read its
magical leaves accompanied only by the
song of the sea's rising tide issuing from
Neptune's throat. The night's air at dusk
consoled me with its sweet, hypnotic voice
& cool embrace under the slate-grey sky
enshrouding Neruda's dark island, & left me staring
in awe as I attempted, in desperation,
to stuff the leaf poems into my coat pocket,
but they crumbled & fell to the ground,
reuniting with the earth that so generously
gave birth to them in the cycle of
that poet's vision.

Shifting Gears

And so here we hold onto one thread
at a time, spun from the delicate litany
of things thought to be done,
as if our balance will remain, as if
the yet undefined truth will balance
everything in this dance with the
macabre, this psychic pugilism with
the unknown, all of us looking for the
Joe Louis hurrahs spiriting through
our hearts, with at least a crowd-pleasing
knockout in the third round.

Holding tight in response to everyday
uncertainties, we have become more
intimate with wobble, but far from
expert, as we croon our hollow tunes
of connection and faux joy
in what has become an altogether common
chorus of pretend togetherness.

Nocturnal Charts

From a distant hill
I've seen fireflies light
the flowering meadow
as dusk sets in.

I've seen motorists drive
without headlights on country
roads as if they were seeking
something in the landscape,
or in the night's clear sky.

After all, some things go better
without light, when the heart's
urgings rev up to decibels
of longing in dark hours.

I've seen evidence of souls
with their delicate wanderings,
there in the quiet of the night
awaiting its kiss of dew—their only
succor as beggars of the night.

There is magic in the air: the stars,
the fireflies, the cars, the errant souls
and the gentle kiss of dew now
enveloping everything, the lonely
roads leading to anywhere.

A Song for Earth from Outer Space

It might be thought that from 248 miles out
the Earth might just look like a fixed, blue
land-speckled globe, or maybe a giant blue-brown
taw poised and ready to reorder the the solar system

On second glance, it really is stunning with its wink to
all the other planets around it. But then,
when the micro view pulls one's attention to all the souls
scampering about in its droughts, it's famine, it's pandemic-
laced imbroglios and strife, the tribal habits of warfare among
virtually all of its people, there is a quiet pause.

The astronauts, privileged enough to glimpse at
our third planet from the Sun, can pause to marvel
at its beauty, and are fortunate during their temporary
high tech detachment from the lunatic conventions
and global realities abounding around the sphere far below them,
the one nestled fixedly, seemingly immobile.

Time is a curious messenger

of facts, slippery slants
of perception, now as I sit
contemplating the colorful, intricate
design of the room's Persian rug, the
black piano, elephant figurines, the
art from India adorning the walls,

all objects of a bona fide earthly nature,
of things as imagined by Lucretius, testaments
of the human spirit, of human endeavor in
sculpture, craft and weave, everything essential,
masterworks shaken loose from their creators,
now transported here before me, tokens
of everything ideal in the heart of things,
gifts of wisdom and integrity,

so that their songs resonate around
a soul.

Threads of a Dream

Chicago's little sister-gem of the Rust Belt,
just up the Lake Michigan shore,
south side church spire-sitter of historic
parochial neighborhoods, one proud basilica, a world class
four-sided clock tower, cradler of a once great
Menomenee tribal culture, home to
beer and iron baron dreams, factories and
German, Polish and Italian immigrants of the
1800s who forged New World hopes over Old World
fates, city of transformation and melting pot experiment,
a city not yet fully defined, merging with the African American,
the Hmong, and the Hispanic imprints of this century—
Milwaukee is wishing, hoping, a historical incubator of
mind-expanding activism and vision—
igniting now towards take-off
to a new century.

Fabula

Loosely strung memories
be they from copper-colored
photos with glimpses of the past,

be they from crumpled, pen-written
scrawling reflecting youthful angst
about love and war and miscellaneous

yearnings, be they reassurances for
loved ones not to worry, that safety
was always at hand, and if not,

guardian angels would appear,
like in the Wim Wenders movie,
Wings of Desire, to salvage any

scrambling, lost souls. But all of those
are but faint memories now, dusty recollections
and best described with care

in metaphor

Some Things

For every person or object, a shadow,
but only with the sun's permission.
For every tide, the moon lends force.

Through nightshades, stars gather dreams
and cast them down upon us, ones we
can fall into, or rise from.

Shorelines give us magical stones
from the Earth's crucible, and, like children
we are enthralled by their shiny, colorful
solid forms.

All part of the world we walk in, we
learn instinctively to savor any light
beamed on black soil that can be,

with some luck someday, a field of
sunflowers lighting our way.

Sphere

Bio
Logical

Eco
Woke

Green forests
Clear streams

Stars winking
In blackness

Hope springs
Forth even in ash

Scars are evidence
That gaping wounds

Can be healed
Souls lifted

Fisherman X

On one end of the pier in Talcahuano,
a fishing village not far from Concepcion, Chile,
fishermen gather around the side of the pier
and a commotion ensues for something being hauled
up onto the pier by another man in a boat. A body,
large and rigid, like a huge fish, is shoved and pulled
headfirst above the lip of the concrete pier. The man's
open eyes seem to stare into the dawn's brightness,
a cruel reality between his night and day,
after he had set out the night before in his trawler
in search of lobster, abalone and sea bass to sell
to the fish mongers for the morning market.

He who caught from the sea was himself claimed,
a trophy catch by the elements of his life to which his body
surrendered unwillingly —perhaps due to a slip, a heart attack,
a trip on his boat enough to send him reeling into the pull of
the cold, black sea. And now, laid out with his sea-worthy
clothing and rubber calf-length boots expelling their slugs
of sea water on the dock, there perhaps mocked by his
enemies, grieved by his friends, in his respite from all
standing above him during his unpredicted ocean-side wake.

One wonders, at moments like these, if there are silent cries
of lost-being and dreams issuing from the corpse's open mouth,
if they recount sweet and harsh memories, if they might be food
for a memoir that will never be.

Sojourn in Panama

There is a sad soulfulness here to behold.
It goes round and round in Spanish sounds
that ricochet off the walls of Casco Viejo
and moseys on down narrow cobblestone streets
with its own special assonance and consonance
echoing in every barrio, mourning a past
of some hidden might-have-been memory
of a nation with wings once its own flesh-pottery of self—
meek, indigenous with a sprinkling of Spaniard—
all called forth now in its unique cultural stew,
simmering in this humid isthmus canal city pot
with its skyscraper teeth gnashing at the liquid
hum above, famed for its ability to connect the world
through its sad, shaken and overtaken
people's heart.

Copper Dream

This is really Neruda's land,
land of *campesinos, rotes, Chile Mierda,*
land if Salvador Allende's spaghetti Western fantasies
of good versus evil amid shadows of gray,
lightness and darkness,
land where social contrast triumphs over social justice.
Clint Eastwood has no idea that he was
a hero of the first freely elected Marxist leader
in Latin America, the man who would be one among many of the
    victims
of Pinochet's slick-holstered Boys.
The dream of Neruda's land
remains connected to me by a thin thread
spun out of dusty memories of my alien status there,
in the land of *campesinos, rotos,* and
Chile Mierda.

Things Said

Can anesthetize the tongue,
Create musical metaphor,
Cajole,
Burn a soul like a hot poker iron,

Kindle love in a lover's heart like
The music from a Gypsy's violin,

Stoke a war and, later,
Entreat peace,

Project blame, admit past sins,
Turn around a life teetering on
The edge of despair,

Raise a child from newborn—
Mentor a new spirit.

Cocoon

There were sixteen spinners in a den of
spiders, each with its own iridescent splendor,
each with its own unique gyration,
signaling it/self/being unlike any other.

It might be said that the key to everything
told and untold resides within each oscillation
therein, forces never before told in any
corner of judgment.

I imagine that spider dreams
all carry within them egg secrets
bursting forth with energy and sense,
tapering only under the influence

of mislaid notions about the limitations of
the creative forces within us all, the
sublime hidden in secret corners
of our psyche, those pregnant and ready
to burst out of their cocoon

to disprove it all.

Song of Graffiti

It is like fresh flowers lovingly placed in a vase,
like free art for an otherwise dull, dreary wall,
like a Japanese garden with raked gravel around
carefully situated stones, like
a blues riff on a saxophone.
It is placed where crime, grit & poverty
rise up like Medusa's snaky locks
in untold ways in seedy tenements where
things are spawned every which way but up.
Graffiti brightens gray steel slabs on trains & walls
in otherwise sad-faced neighborhoods,
rides in like a hero, a savior for those stepped on by
capitalist dreams & Horatio Alger
nightmares. Here's where raucous blue swirls
with red & black out-lined John & Jane Doe figures,
stylized gang tag signatures, yellow & green
& purple geometric stokes create a
most glorious song of the dead rising
from the ashes.

At Dusk

In the fields around us
the pitch of crickets plays out
in the key of D, a quiet whistle,
sweet by the friction of their wings
that means rain as the clouds
above dim the moon and we
are spared lightening and thunder
so that a lesson learned here
is that we are not everything
or grand in this natural refuge
in its gift of a wet embrace. Our
story is but one along with
the other creatures here as
we seek, through a faint light
in the distance, a clue of what
we are going towards.

Under the Microscope

Your hat is in the ring,
there, on top of the sawdust.
Your hat's in the ring
because you willed it
on what seemed to be
a clear, blue-skied day
that beckoned you like
a silken, seductive siren,
sunlit and muse-inspired,
one gripped by a destiny
whispering your name
in ear-catching tones and
all the while deluding you
to believe your decision
was one purely your own.

these dire, barely translatable, times

when to hold up an image
when to stand for that image
even when in your heart you know

it's quaking in unreality
it is something thought to be known but
it is a conniving, pure, invention

something too convenient
something in excess of the rational
something nothing more than self-beneficial

fraudulent in substance
fraudulent in your very being
a fraudulent act that betrays you to the core

to the point that it perplexes you
to the point that you cannot in good conscience connect the dots
to the point that the time frame of your life becomes
untranslatable?

O Say Can You See

In the distance of a dawn's red glare
our Stars and Stripes is unstitching,
unraveling into a myriad of parts,
one might say disintegrating albeit from
what had been an imperfect one Nation
for all, one that has fractured into Red
and Blue constructs, divided cultures
prone to feuding about notions of
freedom, protestant ethic pull-your-own-weight
by your bootstraps, and fundamental things
needed to sustain life on the Planet.

And so, it might be asked, can you see
a day when reason for the common good
will triumph over political shenanigans, over
self-interest and parochially charged visions?
I ask you, can we possibly reunite as a
country of largely exceptional people and
thereby transcend the gravitational pull
of ignorance, prejudice and fear in the course
of our current American nightmare?

Let us recognize that nightmares can be
good for us in the end in that they can
cleanse us of the grime that had so plagued
us in the past and put us in a new
calculus for a better future. Like the little
prince from Antoine de Saint-Exupery's novella,
we just need to learn to decipher the absurdities
we have witnessed, to see life with one's heart
rather than solely with one's eyes.

Just Around the Corner

It is said true things linger—
color-splashed delicate butterfly wings,
hawk swoops, brazen-faced marigolds
straining for sun ray, maple sap waiting to
trickle from tree bark into carefully hung collector cans,
ivy scaling trellised brick walls,

all pulsing to something unknown
in between and around the crashed days,
right through the debris so easily
expelled from chimney stack, sheet-metal
pipe, oxidized iron clump, Big Mac wrappers
and pizza box and toxic dump.

It is said that true things linger inn America-the beautiful,
that our children dance inside it kaleidoscope,
that headache and nightmare can sometimes be touched
by beauty, poise, grace and conscience.

It is said…

Ascent

The clarion call is out:
We must dust ourselves off
from the ashcans of past illusions.
We can and will construct
the seemingly unimaginable,

just as Leonardo da Vinci dreamed
of the bamboo and silk wings with which man
could fly someday,

just as the Dutch
dreamed of and constructed
a brilliant system of dykes and technical
innovations to control and manage
the North Sea that could have inundated their
civilization forever.

From the scary realm
people have/can and will rise
emboldened with the experience
of having fallen, even into the deepest
ashes.

The Dance

There it was.
I'd been missing it all along,
the panhandler in Brooklyn,
in the Latin Quarter in Paris,
on Las Ramblas in Barcelona,
on the streets of Milwaukee,
the boulevards in Hollywood,
amidst the frenetic bustle of Miami,
the dusty hills of Ciudad Juarez,
on Copacabana beach in Rio,
in Santiago, in Port-of-Spain—
the extended hands, the broken
tones of vocal pleas, and oh God,
the eyes, the eyes that watch you
pass by in apparent denial of their need,
as you silently cast your unwilling nod
their way and simply say *"sorry"*
in your transparent waltz in the Republic of
Hypocrisy that is your conscience.

Muted

On the wall of my study hangs a
gift from a now deceased photographer
friend, a reminder, the picture, of the past
that currently looms like a specter of things
never changed, things once given quiet
lip-service over the years. The pain in
the man's face in the photograph
would be worse, undoubtedly, if he
were still alive—I imagine deeper
lines in his furrowed brow and jaw,
perhaps even a more intense glare
in his eyes at the contemporary world
he would be witnessing—after so much
tongue-wagging by all of those he wanted
to trust before to create hope for his
children, maybe grandchildren.

listening

if one listens carefully
amidst the chattering of cicadas after sundown,
other sounds emerge,
scream right through clay-packed earth
and sandy hills, demanding that their voices
be heard, now in these silent, otherwise
lethargic and scary times of the living dead.

the voices are of *the disappeared ones,* once
pushed into death in the fields in Chile,
Argentina, Central America, the Middle East,
Africa, Bosnia—even in America at places
like Wounded Knee, victims of massacres
bred by the lunacy of those bent-on control
by any means over those of other ethnic,
religious and political identities.

listen, on warm summer nights under
starry skies, to how the air quivers with an
unmistakeable vibrato, the chorus of lost souls
wanting only
to return home to what was once theirs.

In the Service of the Symbolic

(for Vincent van Gogh)

Yours is the cry, the absurd, the brilliant
cocaine of pure genius, alone and naked
on a cold-stung hill of solitude that hails us
from the palace halls of the gods, that
expresses the darkness inside
that can be just too much,
the scream of self with its
intense emotions that from your
asylum room cast us in awe into the realm
of *The Starry Night,* and thrust us
into your wavy lines that crackle
with boldness and reject
the idealized harmony of things,
taboo because of your bitter, inner
turmoil, your anger, your painful fusion
with and acceptance of a life less ideal,
your self-portraits shout
a lonesome soul under the threat
of falling into despair and uncertainty
with your visions of the stars
trembling in the night air
in their swirls of seemingly infinite intensity,
and the sun's promise to rise in all its glory.

Life at the Balboa Club Hotel, Mazatlán, Mexico 1973

The Pacific beams bright against
the backdrop of its airy blue shade of sky,
but it does not steal away sadness
from the drifting thoughts that dance
through the clouds on their way to
the horizon. Here one should be happy but...

the mind experiences curious wanderings
into the layered notions of family lost
and buried through the erosion that time—
with its flow—offers without fail. Here I am
needing to pen a letter to a long-lost someone
who has infiltrated my labyrinth of solitude .

Even though they say that Mexican mail does not
move like back home, I will have to be optimistic
that the letter will reach its distant destination,
as I continue to content myself with watching
giant manta rays skim across the skin of the sea
in the relentless afternoon sun.

Reminiscence on a Sunday Afternoon

One sunny fall afternoon I, a man with no name, step out onto the deck to relax. It is an exceptionally quiet day, except for the birds that begin their birdsong without hesitation: I become their audience. After an unknown time there in my trance-like state, I realize that my coming outside today was purpose-driven, that my left hand still clutches the garage door opener I had picked up on the way out. I give it a click. As the garage door opens, it does so with a screeching sound reminiscent of, as best as I can tell, Ennio Morricone's score for *The Good, the Bad and the Ugly:* I am suddenly under the rich blue Almerian sky in Spain where Sergio Leone cranked out that Spaghetti western circa 1966. [Silence]... no bird song. Just a man with no name now transported to the mesquite plains of Almeria, dressed in cowboy garb atop my stallion next to another pale-faced rider—Clint Eastwood—who with piercing blue eyes and a small cigar between his lips, glances over to this man with no mane and say, "Sorry mister, I got to get going...You coming with?" For unknown reasons, I stay put as Clint rides off down the dusty road, his six-shooters blue metal glistening under the Spanish sun. [Blackout]...return to my backyard birdsong. I with no name am seated exactly where I was before, garage opener in hand. The uncertain fate of my garage door is seriously pondered. I pause a moment, but then click the opener impulsively, so I can hear Morricone at least one more time.

Land of Cloudy Water

(from the Dakota Sioux word *Mnisota*)

In a idyllic, hilly farm region,
home to mythic trolls who spooked my

ancestors, sent them spiriting away from
Norway in ships packed stem-to-stern

joining others fleeing the trolls' fiery
curses of famine, gave birth to wide-eyed

enthusiasm, pioneer-dreams
on clusters of land wrenched away

from the Ojibwa and Dakota Sioux
in the Minnesota Territory,

the casualties of a land-grab so
immense that those two formerly

warring tribes were relegated to
reservations by an all-knowing, all-just

American government in the throws
of muscle-building and excluding

anything getting in its way of what
it termed Manifest Destiny, the heart-throb

imprint stamped on the Europeanization
of the land that is now my America, the

land of those ancestors whose choices
saved them from famine and trolls,

but converted them into takers, budgers
of native cultures in the new frontier.

Trading hammers for hatchets, they were
both happy in the beginning.

A Tale

The children have forgotten
everything but the circles in the sand
that bright beach day—

even the pendulum arc of the playground
swings sent flying by the energy of parents'
arms that gave birth to the screams of joy

that radiated from those spaces
in time, from those moments
of the heart of quiet pushes given

to the projectiles of their
fondest dreams, roles
overlooked now in the

cool afternoon air of the season,
its only reminder a fading
glimmer of memory secretly

seeking the azure water again
that lent its forces to create
Its own joy that day on

the beach.

The Wait

Lost bones hang like stones on the necks
of loved ones and ears ring with their cries,
spawning a tragic state of vigilance for the dead
and missing. For many, there can be no real rest

until the remains of the disappeared are uncovered.
Think of Mozart heaped with vagabonds near Vienna,
Lorca with a bullfighter and a teacher just outside of Granada,
not to mention countless lost ones throughout the world. Gone.

Something much worse than mere death, more like Death's
unattainable ransom, seed of grimaced, gothic-like blackened
    faces,
breath and hope like turrets still spiraling toward the blue sky.

Passing

Not of this world but the others,
our origins come atomic and gritty,
a stardust-drawn and blown to an
Earth-land crawl aspiring to
some point of being, of shimmering
elements amidst the nothingness
in imaginary tokens of conjoined
creation,

or so we assume in a continuous bout
with uncertainties, and we adapt and gather
incremental knowledge to guide us into
the Great Dance as things pass from one
to another to another...

And all the while, we spy on and scan
the stars ghosting away above in the
heavens, and with reverence, we secretly
mourn the passing of their magnificence
when we allow ourselves to see them
with the curiosity of a child's heart.

Ice Flow

There brightly under the star-shine
evenings bow in reverence,
earthly things stare in awe,
salt flats sleep deeply,
oceans reflect the nature
of their tides, the moon
smiles on its kinship with its galaxy—
one of one hundred plus billions of others—
desert sands blow with gentle breath
across the Earth's vast parched face
while the blind keep marching on
under Newton's thought cloud.

Reverie

The stars—the very same ones
that I imagine beheld by my wide-eyed
German and Norwegian ancestors in the
early 1800s—now shine on me, brightly
as they did then in the Midwestern north
country where those relatives built sod-houses
on their tracts of land with their calloused hands,
sweat-soaked and with grunting determination, not
too far from where I, some time and distance later,
sit watching Shakespeare under that same canopy
of stars, a smile of wonder on my face while caught up
in the intrigue of the Bard's play, the cicada serenade,
the late summer cool caress off night air—
a communion with something
not totally known there.

Night Shadows

At night dreams
rise and fall like
nebulous memories
desirous of my awareness

fluids passing within my
soul, ghosts perhaps
calling out to me, cords
from some interstellar space,

doing a special dance pastiche
full of disconnected steps
leading to slaps of rhythm
that most mock my night.

I rock in my boat on my back,
staring up at stars whose dust
eons ago ignited the spark that
send me careening here to

this roll of ocean sea, so
insignificant on the scale
of everything around this
rocking boat of bedtime
mysteries with its collage
of pain, illusions of love,
and soul-filling surge.

Pine Forest Ramble

Children trudge through the magical swamplands
of their imagination, along red-clay walls that border
dreamy creeks whose only native intruders are an
occasional water moccasin, crawdads and armies of
shimmering minnows thought to some day become toothy
fish to behold in awe. The hours left lead to exploring paths
where tigers with growly, snarly faces were said to prowl
in search of children such as these, truly wild beasts, both,
during their daily reconnaissance of underbrush, of
emerald-hued patches bordering pine forests,
electrical towers to be climbed as if they were the
Kilimanjaro's of that childhood realm. And then, of course,
all the colorful birds to fall prey to BB shot, stilled
prematurely by the would-be children sharpshooters,
future men boosted with testosterone bursts and sure-shot,
and scoped rifles.

burnt roses

the picture is of a mother
doting on the young child
she is hugging, the child smiling
with the look of promise in his eyes,
the one his mother wishes for him,

a nice child, bright faced
looking into the future with his
child's vision, his mother in
rapture with the promise of it all.

the mother is all around the world,
Iran, Ecuador, Syria, Ukraine, Mozambique,
Chile, et cetera. It doesn't matter where because
it is just the global, parental hand of love

no matter what the child may become, the
love of mother for child is omnipresent,
universal even though at times the power lords
of the world do not judge it so, and some of those
children may grow up into men somehow

installed in unimaginably grotesque lives
filled with the bullet-holes of poverty
and dead end lives—religious pawns
to the King of something malicious—
an unfortunate affiliation, a snare with

a seeming lock on everything that
casts them into the projectiles that
carry them so far from the child in
the picture, the one that had once
so warmed their mothers' hearts.

On the Glade Near Strawberry Fields

We huddled and cried together,
looking up at the moon
on a starry, autumn night.

We prayed with frantic but
unquestionable devotion to
a God who seemed, in the end,
not to hear.

We held hands in a field of
leaf-shrouded grass while birds sang
their irrepressible bird songs.
And nothing changed.

Now, we have grown hoarse
from suppressed screams
that now only find outlet in
repetitive, guttural intonations
as we keep asking why and go on
imagining.

On a Hot Afternoon in Jerusalem

The sun-parched face of an old Arab
crowned with a kaffiyeh,
his nicotine-stained fingers clutching
a smoking Gauloise,
peers directly at the
photographer.

Is this a survivor of untold losses,
of so many blood-curdling mourning wails
of Arab women,
this very same man who sips black coffee
sugared to taste from a demitasse,
a sweet companion to his cigarette,
a sure soothing balm for desperate souls
in such toxic war-torn environments,
here during a sweltering afternoon in the
calmer, narrow lanes of a Jerusalem souk
where Arabic words dance between
walls, then flee, muted, into the open air?

Does he dream too—that Allah
will some day
silence
gunfire forever?

Showdown

So, I pull up to a stoplight
in the city next to a leather-clad
biker with what looks like stubble
at least five days old. He throttles his
Harley Hog in neutral, blasting its engine's
throaty solo roar against everything around it.
The motorcycle and its rider are spontaneous
mavericks among all the plebes around them
who inconspicuously eye it with that
peculiar admix of distain and admiration
epidemic in such social gatherings, but we are taken
by that I-don't-take-no-shit roar of
motorcycle pipes as its rider peels
out in front of me from a dead-stop,
clinching the daytime deal at the stoplight
impromptu showdown there in then shadows
of towering warehouse red-bricks numb to
the happenings below.

On the Road to Mayo

The road itself across Wisconsin, then the western banks of the
Mississippi River consoled us — we took backroads — a scenic,
snail-paced journey devoid of numbing interstate rushing and
bug-spattered windshield. Mick Jagger rocked us with
Satisfaction while we both took in the sights on the winding
drive along the river, going north on the Iowa and Minnesota sides,
stopping briefly to watch a bald eagle glide into a majestic dive to
snatch a large fish from the water. The riverside bluffs on both
sides loomed like stoic, timeless guardians of the river treasure
flowing below. We stopped to admire prairie flowers a little farther
up the winding road, crossed the flat, black-earthed Minnesota
farm fields and drove on through the rolling prairie land until we
finally entered the Rochester city limits. Famished, we found a
roadside cafe where we prided ourselves in ordering and devouring
greasy cheeseburgers and sipped malted shakes, just like we did
when we were love-struck grad students many moons ago. I
couldn't resist the old juke box there so I slipped two quarters in
the slot. As Jagger sang *You Can't Always Get What You Want*,
in the distance we could see Mayo puncturing the late afternoon
sky, a place full of busy magicians in that Mecca of hope, now
shimmering in that ever so reachable distance before us.

The Call

Freedom
Free-do
Freedom dumb
Free to live life
  too free
Free to choose
Free to fail-fall
  with "freedom"
Free to stand
  on principles
Free to assume
Free to deny
  others their due
  freedom &
  equality
With freedom
A noble concept
But missing
A real logic, siding up
  & cosy with Darwin's
  notions too freely
  in freedom
The kingdom
Of detriment disguised

In Style

I've seen them all along: the needy, statuesque figures with fingers curled, the lone figures except for the others like them, the ones with the same addiction, pariahs in their own right, they stand, a quick gaze here or there at other passers-by, at cars that speed by, at glassed-in buildings even on the coldest and the hottest days. There they are sustained by their hits, as smoke billows from their lips during their legally-imposed sojourns, their acts of compliant isolation cheered on by the ghost of the Marlboro Man. To those in the clouds among us, death by smoke is gusto-seeking, macho, sexy-cool. The unwitting Bogart and Bacall oozed the seductive amalgam of sex and smoke; Cooper, Lana Turner, Nat King Cole and Billie-who-sang-the-blues were all victims of the fashionable trends concocted by admen clever enough to sell fate in cellophane-covered, colorful packs of good life allure.

Quest

Under the starry net cast above
is the full-blown gladness of a Beethoven symphony
on a midsummer's night.
Here all is spoken in images at the juncture
of the lucid and the luminous where
transcendence pulls one into infinity,
where logic and pattern and ethereal
matters duel under impermanent stars
on slow-burn,
where the bioluminescent glow of fireflies
catch and hold the imagination along
with quiet majesty of cedar and poplar trees,
beach rose, mounds of moss—
where Nature is in her glory even through
the surreal fog of afternoon.
We are all made of star-stuff. (Let us not deceive
ourselves: At least ten percent of all stars have
at least one habitable planet,) dollops of rock
in perpetual time-slide,
and we strive to content ourselves
in the silky silence of our third planet from the Sun,
and amid Nature in her glory,
we inhale, we exhale.

The Privileged Secrets of the Arch

Of all of those in the park, only
the rosy-cheeked, disheveled woman saw the
poltergeists weave under and
around the monumental park arch, so much
so that she dropped her plastic bag
filled with everything she owned
and cherished, thereby setting her
hands free to applaud them as they
set about in their anarchistic abandon
magically whirling debris with whistling sounds,
creating traces of colored lines that were
utterly magnificent for this lone observer
to behold. What a shame—she thought—
that she must relish in this free performance
art alone. And how blessed she considered herself
that only she could enjoy such a gift in her
own dusty, litter-strewn amusement park while
others there could content themselves with just
simply staring at her.

On Stargazing

Today I wash my hands
as if to insure a clean tender touch
as if to scramble or nullify
any coup against the image
of fresh life flower held and so coveted
    in secret moments
during dawn breaking the night
as if paper can be saved from fire
as if I can tilt at misunderstood
windmills without a less romantic better half
as if answers can come with Sisyphean effort
as if the sounds of solitude will calm me
as if forever...

Going to Visit a Dying Friend

The road there seems long
with the roadblocks of thought
that creep and lie in wait,
like potholes and detour signs
wanting to mess with me,
as I try at every turn to focus
on the purpose of this trip,
a pilgrimage to rescue and comfort
a soul longing to cling to hope.
I swallow hard trying to forget my own
long-standing separation issues
that are cruelly fingering me with a sense of
ineptitude and challenge me to
rise up in martyrdom to the cause.
But Deep down I know I will glide
into the expected role, the one cast
by a director of the unknown now
taking a foolish chance on me.

The Ancient Art of War in the Garden

The Greek mint has begun its ruckus again in the backyard.
I have tried to teach it to lower its voice, but it has paid no heed.

A Japanese maple, rose of Sharon tree and a flash of flowering
    bushes,
while maintaining social distance, have been cringing but tolerant.

The cedar board deck, aged and grayed by its years, yet handsome
and commanding, serves as a mute border to the proliferating
    garden growth

that is really, admittedly the hub of color-swirl and herbal takeover
there. A copper wind sculpture, faded green and with its double
    helix

patterns formed by the gratis compliment of wind on a spectrum
from low—high, can only co-exist, a metal figurine to be toyed
    with

by the weather, subservient but oh so enduring and statuesque. And
all the while, the aggressive Greek mint's roots wrestle with its

adjoining herbal brothers and sisters, and won't allow for a
three-count during its battle for soil nutrients, fierce

and ruthless like Achilles conquering Hector there in my
suburban garden, a veritable Troy to that race of one

undeniably aromatic, Greek herb, its only *heel* being
vulnerable to the trowel shelved and waiting in the garage.

Word in my house is that its fate will be not death,
but solitary confinement in a yard pot in a remote, distaff

section of the rock ecosphere there.

Snow During a Visit to Kalamazoo

These snowy woods in Kalamazoo,
full of oak, hickory, cedar and ash trees
standing like sturdy pale ghosts against the
snow and gray sky, evoke the wonder of
all that is transitory, of all that we just can't
understand fully, of our need to grasp
the meaning that still eludes us,
leaving us breathless and in awe, its
raw beauty our only consolation.
And then, the enigma of the twelve-point buck,
rumored by our friends to grace these woods outside
their home with his harem of doe, but who
does not make an appearance despite our
longing that he do so. We could only imagine
the buck's proud trot, head held high, oblivious
to his following doe, those of us awaiting
with eagerness just one glimpse.

The Beast

Ever so often
it can be spotted—
the solitary,
scraggly coyote cutting
through neighborhoods
wherever it is called by some
mysterious force of nature. It
invariably gets no respect:
Unsympathetic drivers honk their horns,
neighborhood dogs bark their warnings
and kids think maybe that it'd be cool
if the beast intruder could only be
hit by a passing car, so they could get
a closer look, maybe kick it or something.

Seeing all of this makes me side in secret
with the perceived pariah, as I follow him in his
determined saunter down our street while he looks for
God knows what, like a bestial Quixote
on a secret mission to restore some natural
order in this, our world together.

A Midnight Soiree in Paris

The musical entertainment in a bar in Paris changed around
midnight. No sooner had the opening combo left when in
came the new bass player accompanied by a saxophonist,
a drummer and a trumpeter. Nothing unusual were it not for
the fact that, as they took their positions on stage, it became
clear that the bass player was a giant panda, the saxophonist
a giraffe, the drummer a black-maned lion, and the trumpet
player a hippopotamus. Despite the initial shock, when the
music started the whole place was hypnotized. Putting it
mildly, the music was electrifying and no one cared a bit
that the musicians were, well, so unusual, not to forget the
duende that oozed from an enchanting chanteuse —
a leopard in a ruffled black frock who rendered soulful
songs Billie Holiday style.

Another surprise came about half way through the new set
when in ran a tiger who whipped a conch out of a bag and
blew a wild accompaniment for the rest of the evening that
fired up the group into a musical frenzy that inspired the place
to dance the evening away, until all were sated and the joint
closed. It was a matter of a new type of band and the magical
music it played that drove everyone euphoric before the night
club closed, and forced us to walk away into the balmy
night air on a mission to decipher the enigma of that
more-than-fabulous evening.

That Day

Today I sit in the darkness
of my expected loneliness,

not without a sigh, not
without the shiver that

does not hesitate to grab you
during the solitary screenshots

arising in your imagination, those
vivid ones that shadow your wounded

soul, the one that has only sought harmony
in the wake of all starry nights and days

festooned with flowers and laughter,
all of which now are but transient

glimpses of what once was,
mere ghosts of day and night.

Primogenitor

Time was when billets-doux were
handwritten with Mont Blanc pens,

those elegant instruments full of the
graceful art of expression

coupled with beautiful hieroglyphic signs
conveying the ultimate
in thoughts, dreams and love.

Now assignations are typed,
they are boringly uniform regimented little offspring
of their glorious grandparents.

I long for a renaissance of the fluid, curved
s, sensuously shaped j, beautiful b, infinite o,

exotic but rare z, occasional and mysterious
x, kinky y, and their 19 other siblings,

all whispering with life, mainlined so artfully
to the should with the pizzazz óf pen point.

Halloween, 2019 in Brooklyn

Today, there really is something magical about Darth Vader
& Luke Sky Walker crossing one another's paths in full costume
& regalia here in Park Slope. When they meet, albeit somewhat
comical to the onlooker, their encounter is real play action scripted
by the power of imagination some light years from their parents
who lag behind diligently in a mixed state of faded Trekkie images
with a modicum of curiosity salvaged perhaps by the paper cup of
Starbucks-something in their hand, trolling behind, missing the
sparks generated when Darth's & Luke's fluorescent swords strike
against one another & bring civilization closer to full circle,
righting what's wrong in each in a glorified gesture of believing
in good & evil. Beyond the candy they score by the end of the
evening, the Force is with them both as the ragtag ghosts, goblins
& vampires flank them to the right & left, with their own bevy
of dazed-faced parents moseying close behind.

looking for seashells

the sand hides part of their
depth, the color and patterns
of their sea-made exoskeletons
of calcium carbonate shelter
created by a delicate array of
creatures vulnerable to the
ecosystems that support them.

their discovery on beaches is
a joy for us, especially for the
curious children who pluck them
from their sandy beachheads as
joyful discoveries which become
bedroom collections for those
whose imaginations fuel dreams

of the sea, fantasies of Jacque Cousteau-
like affiliation deciphering the ocean's
boundless mysteries aboard the Calypso,
sailing into the dangerous escape offered
by breakers that slam seawater onshore
so that seashells, spike-over-crown, are tossed
into the sandy beaches there, jetsam from its depths
that showcase its truth with its glistening frame
of beach sand.

To a Leaf

I, like you, am changed by age,
    curled at the edge, bent forth,
    humbled by the force of wind.
I shift around from one place to another,
    seek out new harmonies with Nature
in all her seeming fickleness through
the seasons. We both are mysteriously
drawn to her tune, ready to do our
similar yet unique jigs
    every time.

Open Lane

the hazel eyes are fixed
on me

and I join his fixed stare
and smile

to hide the tears welling up
while he

almost childlike seems to
make an effort

but his attempt to return
my smile

is intercepted, enfeebled
and fades

and I say *show me how,
dad,* and

in just a tremor of his eyes
his gaze is goodbye,

and the only words that
don't fail me

are *till we meet again
Bob.*

The Bearable Light of Invisibility

The man in the shower couldn't help but notice several hard points
as he lathered his underarm area, first on his right side, then his left
side. Overcome with curiosity, he instinctively scratched the
layered skin around them with his fingernails. His efforts to rid
himself of them continued, shower after shower, but all proved
futile. His thoughts about the curious bodily changes were at first
amusing, to say the least, but eventually the reality of his plight
caused him to think in ways he never suspected he was capable of.
A veritable parade of bizarre thoughts cascaded down upon him.
Thoughts like was he growing wings of his own, certainly unlike
Icarus who had to make his own out of bamboo and silk, or if he
was being transformed into a facsimile of *Birdman* like that
portrayed by Michael Keaton in the movie of that same name?
Maybe too, he wondered if the forces at hand in life itself were
casting him to become a creature like one of the angels conjured up
by Rainer Maria Rilke, the Bohemian-Austrian poet, whose poetry
inspired Wim Wenders' movie, *Wings of Desire*. The man
pondered the above, and concluded that, if he had to choose, that if
he did eventually change into some winged creature, that he
become one of those all-knowing, beneficent angels like those in
the Rilke-inspired Wenders movie, an angel of mercy, invisible but
able to comfort those in distress. The man concluded such a new
chapter in his life, that of a silent hero capable of rescuing the
otherwise tortured souls comprising humanity, would be well
worth his conversion discomfort. Thereafter, instead of scratching
at the hollow horny shafts as they began to emerge from his sides
with increasing semblance to feathers, he stroked them gently as if
they were becoming his wings of hope. After all, he concluded,
immortality is bound to have a price.

In Memory of the Night Before

Never will I know what my mother thought
that last day of light in her life, there
in her hospital bed when she hugged
my sister and me, her sadness disguised
by her radiant smile, all the while things
in her life were shape-shifting into coldly
broadcast matters of fact, where the surrender
required of her on that dark Christmas Eve
there in Marietta, Georgia, simply because
things had to be that way, leaving us all
devoid of her company on that joyless
morning of Christ's birth.

Since then, I have upon occasion pondered
the state of affairs in these lives we all lead,
and have concluded that there is nothing much
there beyond the day-to-day joys, the episodes
of wonder, the daily whispers of concern
we share with one another in the mysterious tunnels
of life that we must inevitably travel through, the
ultimate challenge—to recognize
and marvel at the beauty of those things
we encounter along the way that, in their
own way, pass us by like fireflies in the night.

Day Token

It was a city
chased by ideas
& dreams

It is place of
loneliness & dislocation
now

where drab buildings
mold souls into escape
fantasies, into

the realm of imaginary
forests of lithograph-like
trees that fade

into gray, gnarled phantoms
of themselves as they
envelope the figure

who imagines them in
journeys through days
of darkness.

The Post

There it is, then, the
bartering trade of thought,
the arc of dissonance,
a divide of things where
plasticity has failed its
task of stretching concepts
making divisive notions
collide in the fog of not knowing
what is real and not real, torching
what were once fond emotions,
melting them into cinders,
casualties of the moment,
left alone to smolder
into their own ash that
will mourn what once was,
what may not ever be
anything like before.

Fashion

In the dream
I was clad in
the cool wrap
of 8 mil enforced
coextrusion polyethylene
with a straight zipper,
no handle straps, feeling
truly stylish in that state,
having arrived...having
arrived in the modest
fashion of the moment,
and when I woke...

the forge

america is a newborn loaded up
with notions of democratic grandeur
yet-to-mature, america is every
sweat-john & jane doe
treading on its backbone trying to find
their own song, america is everything
to Lady Liberty, but shift-shaped nightmares
to most of the people pounding its streets,
america is the victim of historical spasms of
hypocrisy, people being dislocated from land
to land by others locating on that land, america
has had its share of vile corruption that has
rotted our roots, america is contented customers,
with its Fords, Chevys, Oldsmobiles, Coca Cola
& Marlboros, rich oil & gas & coal & lest we forget
steel companies that all built this hulking, guzzling
juggernaut phenomenon that still is a home & isn't a home
to its huddled masses, those good-faith immigrants
sprung far & wide with constitutionally-derived
notions from the framers of this novice, upstart
nation that has rewarded only those who
circle up their wagons to fend off any perceived
adversity, america is children hiding under their
school desks to avoid death by gunfire, america
is a child of change but doesn't yet know it, america
has become divided, like it or not, into distinct blue
& red territories, primed & prepped for a clash,
a fragmentation of brothers & sisters, family & friends,
a condition of cultish, cultural clash very apt to bleed
america into a moribund coma, not unlike that of a
terminally-ill child still dreaming like Horatio Alger
to someday become whole.

Aftermath

Forever is never.
Hope is a token elixir.

Centuries do not
muffle delusion.

Never can call too often.
Sunrises are Nature's makeup

flowing into yet another day.
This is how the soul moves,

in the current of the stars
that shine radiantly,

a chorus to our longing,
our love of star stuff.

It's an illusion of breath
in our finer

moments.

The Swerve

Things just work out that way sometimes.
Jarring and jagged cut-you-up things
    that spring up from the least expected places.
The sharp-toothed jackal that comes in the shadows
    of the day to take away someone you love,
the disappointment by a friend who you had
    so cherished before,
the dream shattered by a slight-minded person
    in power unmoved by your light-source,
and then, and then the action taken by your
    own hand that is self-or-other-betraying
in its blanket lust, its perception far afield
    from the bullseye of truth in the matter at hand.

All of this is ski-jawed freewill in the house of
    destiny,
where we must do the high wire balancing act
    above the bigtop circus, and lest we forget,
there is a world watching our every bob and weave,
    a world that expects us to put on a good show
in spite of the shaky, thin wire we all must tread.

About the Author

Stephen Anderson is a Milwaukee poet/writer and translator whose work has appeared in *Southwest Review, Blue Heron Review, Tipton Poetry Journal, New Purlieu Review, Free Verse, Verse Wisconsin, Poetica Review, Foundling Review, Poetry Hall, Verse-Virtual, Latin American Literature Today,* the anthology *Poems to Lift You Up & Make You Smile,* as well as in other online and print journals. His poetry has been featured on the Milwaukee NPR-affiliate WUWM Lake Effect Program. He is the author of three chapbooks, and two full-length collections, *In The Garden Of Angels And Demons (2017), and The Dream Angel Plays The Cello (2019.)* Several of his poems appeared in the poetry collection, *Portals And Piers* (2012). In the summer of 2013, six of his poems formed the text for a chamber music composition entitled *The Privileged Secrets of the Arch* performed by some musicians, including two members of the Milwaukee Symphony Orchestra and an opera singer. His experiences while living abroad as a Peace Corps Volunteer in Chile, and in London, England when he taught at the University of London/ Queen Mary and Westfield College have influenced his writing in that it tends to be more globally-focused rather than purely regional. His work is being archived under the Stephen Anderson Collection in the Raynor Libraries at Marquette University.

www.ingramcontent.com/pod-product-compliance
Lightning Source LLC
Chambersburg PA
CBHW020232090426
42735CB00010B/1660